# Who Sank the Boat?

*To my mother*
*Esma Griffiths*

First published in Australia in 1983

First published in this edition 1989 by Maurbern Pty Ltd

Reprinted 1990

Copyright © Thomas Nelson Australia 1983

Distributed in the United States by
RIGBY INC
PO Box 797
Crystal Lake Illinois 60014

ISBN 0 7327 0185 6

Printed in Hong Kong

# Who Sank the Boat?

Pamela Allen

**RIGBY**

Beside the sea, on Mr Peffer's place, there lived

a cow, a donkey, a sheep, a pig,
and a tiny little mouse.

They were good friends,
and one warm sunny morning,
for no particular reason,
they decided to go
for a row in the bay.

Do you know who sank the boat?

Was it the cow
who almost fell in,
when she tilted the boat
and made such a din?

No, it wasn't the cow
who almost fell in.

Do you know who sank the boat?

Was it the donkey
who balanced her weight?
Who yelled,
'I'll get in at the bow before it's too late.'

No, it wasn't the donkey
who balanced her weight.

Do you know who sank the boat?

Was it the pig
as fat as butter,
who stepped in at the side
and caused a great flutter?

No, it wasn't the pig
as fat as butter.

Do you know who sank the boat?

Was it the sheep
who knew where to sit
to level the boat
so that she could knit?

No, it wasn't the sheep
who knew where to sit.

Do you know who sank the boat?

Was it the little mouse,
the last to get in,
who was lightest of all?

Could it be him?

You DO know who sank the boat.